# Your Amazing
## Itty Bitty™
# Business Tax Book

*15 Simple Tips for Saving Money*
*On Your Taxes!*

Deborah A. Morgan, CPA

Published by Itty Bitty™ Publishing
A subsidiary of S & P Productions, Inc.

Printed in the United States of America

Itty Bitty™ Publishing
311 Main Street, Suite E
El Segundo, CA 90245
(310) 640-8885


ISBN: 978-1-931191-59-3

*Dedicated to Paul, Richard, and Robert*

# Table of Contents

# Tip 1
## Business Entities

Before you start your business, it's important to understand the different business entity types.

1. The most popular entity types for small business owners are the following:
   a. Sole Proprietorship
   b. Limited Liability Company (LLC)
   c. C Corporation
   d. S Corporation
2. Sole proprietorship is the easiest to form. This is opened by simply starting your business. There is no separate tax return filing requirement. An item of note, net income is subject to self-employment tax.
3. LLCs are formed by filing with your State. Whether you file as a sole proprietorship, partnership, or corporation is dependent upon the number of members (owners) you have and the way they choose to be taxed.
4. Corporations are also formed by filing with your State. The primary difference between the C Corporation and the S Corporation is how they are treated for tax purposes. Most small business owners choose to be an S Corporation rather than a C Corporation.

**Things To Consider When Choosing A Business Entity:**

- Will you be a sole owner?
- Do you plan on taking your company public?
- How much income do you anticipate making?
- How does your State tax the LLC? All States are taxed differently. This may help determine which entity to choose.

# Tip 2
## Ordinary and Necessary Expenses

According to the Internal Revenue Code Section 162 – There shall be allowed as a deduction all the **ordinary** and **necessary** expenses paid or incurred during the taxable year in carrying on any trade or business.

1. An *ordinary* expense is an expense that is common and accepted in your business. Examples of ordinary expenses are rent and office supplies.
2. A *necessary* expense is an expense that is helpful and appropriate in your business. An example of necessary expenses is body oil for a body builder. Of course, assuming the body builder is a business.
3. In order for any business expense to be allowed, you must be operating the business as a business to make a profit and not as a hobby.

**Things To Consider About Ordinary And Necessary Expenses:**

- Do you use it normally for your business?
- Is it required for your business?
- If it is an unusual expense, can you prove that it helps your business if audited?
- Make sure you have documentation for the expense.

# Tip 3
## Auto Expenses

Auto expenses are very common. However, many people are unaware that there are two ways you can determine the deduction for auto expenses. There is the *standard mileage rate method* or the *actual expense method*.

1. The *standard mileage rate method* is the deduction taken when you calculate your business mileage and multiply that by the current year's standard mileage rate, which is set by the Internal Revenue Service and is adjusted periodically.
2. The other option you can use to deduct auto expenses is the *actual expense method*.
    a. This method also requires that you calculate the business miles driven and the total miles driven for the year.
    b. The business miles are then compared to the total miles driven to come up with a business use percentage.
    c. You can deduct the business use percentage of auto expenses such as gas, insurance, repairs, lease payments, interest, etc.

**Things to Consider About Auto Expenses:**

- You should not assume that one method is better than the other.
- Both methods require good recordkeeping for miles driven so it is important to develop a method to track your business mileage.
- Commuting miles (going from your home to your office) is not considered business mileage.

# Tip 4
## Home Office Deduction

You are allowed to take a home office deduction if it is your principal place of business and a place you use regularly and exclusively in the normal course of your business. There are two methods for deducting a home office deduction: the *regular method* and the *simplified method*.

1.  The *regular method* is calculated by taking the business square footage area divided by the total square footage of the home.

    Once you compute the business percentage, you can then deduct the business percentage of rent or mortgage interest, property taxes, insurance, utilities, etc.

2.  The *simplified method* is a standard deduction of $5 per square foot of the home used for the business up to a maximum of 300 square feet.

**Things To Consider About Your Home Office
Deduction:**

- Do not be afraid to take a home office
  deduction. If you really have a home office
  deduction, take it. Some think this is an
  automatic cause for an audit, it is not.
- Both methods require that you calculate the
  square footage of your home office area.
- When using the simplified method, you can
  take the full mortgage and property tax
  deductions on Schedule A (Itemized
  Deductions), rather than allocating a
  percentage to Schedule A and a percentage to
  the business home office portion.
- Calculate both methods to see which works
  better for your situation.

# Tip 5
## Retirement Plans

Retirement contributions are a great way to save money on your taxes for business owners. It is also highly recommended because most business owners have the responsibility of planning for their own retirement.

1. There are many retirement plan options. The most popular plans for small business owners are:
   a. Simplified Employee Pension Plan - SEP IRA
   b. Savings Incentive Match Plan for Employees – SIMPLE IRA
   c. Self Employed 401(k) Plan
2. Each plan offers different tax savings benefits such as:
   a. Receiving a tax credit when starting the plan.
   b. The ability to deduct employer contributions.
   c. Deferred tax growth potential without paying current taxes on current growth.

**Things To Consider When Choosing
Retirement Plans:**

- Each plan has its own benefits. Speak to a financial advisor about which one is right for your business.
- Do you have employees that you want to include in the plan?
- Will you need access to the funds before retirement age?
- Are you looking for a plan with large contribution limits?

# Tip 6
**Employees and Independent Contractors**

Many business owners like to say that their "workers" are independent contractors rather than employees.

1. Selecting the incorrect classification / treatment of your "workers" can cause penalties and aggravation.
2. If an employee is incorrectly classified as an independent contractor, you will be liable for payroll taxes in addition to the related penalties and interest.
3. The main distinction between an employee and independent contractors is control.
   a. An individual is generally an *independent contractor* if they have the right to control when and how something will be done.
   b. An *employee* is someone that you direct when and how something will be done. You set their hours, you supervise their work, and provide their tools.

**Things To Consider When Deciding Between
Employees and Independent Contractors:**

- Does the "worker" have other clients?
- Does the "worker" have a license for their business?
- Does the "worker" determine the timing of when their task is required to be completed?
- If you answered yes to the questions above, the "worker" is probably an independent contractor.

# Tip 7
## Cash / Accrual Basis

There are two ways of tracking business income and expenses. These methods are *cash basis* and *accrual basis*. Accounting software will usually ask what basis of accounting you are on.

1.  *Cash basis* takes place when you record income when the cash is actually received. Expenses are recorded when the expense is actually paid.

    Individuals are almost always on the cash method of accounting.

2.  *Accrual basis* is when companies report income when the income is earned. For example, an attorney may report income when an invoice for services has been billed. Likewise, expenses are reported when the expense is incurred rather than when paid.

**Things To Consider About Cash / Accrual Basis:**

- It is beneficial to be able to run your financial statements on both the cash and accrual basis.
- The accrual basis gives you the opportunity to see who owes you and who you owe.
- *Bad debt* is not a write-off for taxpayers because they are on the cash basis of accounting. This is because while you may have done work for someone and they did not pay you, you did not actually have an outlay of cash for your services.

# Tip 8
## Meals and Entertainment

Like all business expenses, meals and entertainment must be ordinary and necessary. However, there are additional items that need to be documented in order to deduct meals and entertainment. The expense must meet one of the two tests – it must be *directly-related* or *associated*.

1. The *directly-related* test primarily states that the combined business and entertainment activity had business conducted, you engaged in business during the entertainment period, and you had a general expectation of a business benefit in the future.
2. If your meals and entertainment do not meet the directly related test, it needs to meet the *associated test*. The associated test means the meal and entertainment was associated with your business and was before or after a business discussion.
3. Meals and entertainment are generally only allowed to be deducted at 50%.

**Things To Consider About Meals and Entertainment:**

- Meals and entertainment need to be documented with extra support such as who you met with, what the purpose of the meeting was, and where did you meet?
- If you are audited, the IRS will require additional information other than just the receipt that proves the payment.
- Does the expense also qualify under the IRS ordinary and necessary expense requirement?
- Entertainment expenses for spouses are generally not deductible unless there is a clear business purpose.

# Tip 9
## Fixed Assets and Depreciation

Fixed assets are items that are purchased for use in the day-to-day operations of your business such as computers and equipment. Fixed assets are considered assets rather than an expense because the use of the asset generally provides benefits for more than one year.

1. Depreciation is the "writing off" process of an asset over its useful life. For simplicity sake, assume office furniture is purchased for $7,000 and has a useful life of seven years. Depreciation expense will be recorded at $1,000 per year for seven years. This is calculated by dividing the purchase price over the number of useful life years.

2. When you sell an asset that has been depreciated, the value of the asset is the net of depreciation. For example, if you purchased the asset for $7,000 and have taken $2,000 in depreciation, the basis of the asset is $5,000 when determining whether you have a gain or loss on the sale of the asset. If you sell the asset for $8,000, your gain is $3,000.

The IRS Section 179 depreciation allows full depreciation of the asset during the first year but is subject to dollar certain limitations.

**Things To Consider About Fixed Assets and Depreciation:**

- Find out what the current year limit of Section 179 depreciation is for the year that you are filing your tax returns. You may be allowed to depreciate the asset in full the first year it is purchased.
- If you are a sole proprietor, you may not take Section 179 depreciation if you have a loss.
- When selling an asset be sure you have the current basis (actual cost less depreciation previously taken plus any improvements made).
- Be sure to maintain a depreciation schedule for all assets.

# Tip 10
## Accurate Accounting Records

Having good accounting and bookkeeping records will help you be in control of your business and provide a clear understanding of your success.

1. There are many other benefits of having accurate accounting records, including:
   a. You will be well prepared at tax time because you already have your accounting completed.
   b. Accurate accounting records will most likely save you money on your tax preparation fees.
   c. In the event of an audit, your accounting records will already be completed and you will be able to support everything on your returns.
   d. You will have a great foundation for tax planning and goal setting.
2. More importantly, you will know how you are doing at all times and can make changes as you go along rather than have unexpected financial surprises.

**Things to Consider About Accurate Accounting Records:**

- Take the time to learn how to do your own bookkeeping or outsource this task.
- Maintaining your accounting system throughout the year and not just at year-end is how you can take advantage of the system and plan your business growth.
- There are many accounting software companies that cater to various industries. Seek out the one that is right for your industry.
- I recommend that you hire someone to do the accounting for you. This will typically save you time and money in the long run.

# Tip 11
## Cash and Credit Cards

Cash and credit cards are acceptable forms of payment for business transactions.

1. Be sure to keep receipts and support for all cash and credit card transactions.
2. Although the credit card statements have neatly detailed listing of expenses, you will still be required to show invoices supporting the charges similar to the support that would be required for checks in an audit.
3. Receipts can be digitized and is accepted by the Internal Revenue Service.
4. The timing of expenses on credit cards is a little tricky for tax purposes. You are allowed to use the date of the charge on your credit card statement instead of the date the credit card was paid.

**Things To Consider About Cash and Credit Cards:**

- Create a system for keeping cash and credit card receipts together such as a monthly envelope or folder for reference when you are working on your accounting and taxes.
- Keep track of your daily operations. It is possible that you are spending cash for business items that are not being tracked for business. For example, coffee with a potential client or a trip to the post office to mail something via certified mail.

# Tip 12
### Inventory and Cost of Goods Sold

Inventory are items that are held for sale in the ordinary course of business. These can be items that are purchased and sold or items that are manufactured and sold. Examples include the manufacturing of beauty products, building computers and the sale of clothing.

1. Inventory is considered an asset rather than an expense. Purchasing inventory cannot be written off in the year of purchase.
2. The best way to account for inventory is to treat all purchases as an asset.
3. Once you sell inventory, you take the item away from the asset and record it as cost of goods sold which is a deduction from income.
4. At year end, you should have a physical inventory count to verify that the asset is correct.

**Things To Consider About Inventory and Cost of Goods Sold:**

- Businesses that create inventory *must* track all parts of the inventory. Take clothing, for example. The cost of labor, along with fabric and buttons, should be included as part of inventory.
- Create an inventory worksheet / checklist as you are buying inventory so that you have a standard list as you grow your inventory. This list can be used for your year-end inventory count.
- When selecting accounting software, be sure the software has the capability to track inventory. Not all programs have this feature.

# Tip 13
## Start Up Costs

Start up costs are the costs of setting up a business or investigating in the potential business for purchase or creation.

1.  Many people believe that start up costs prior to starting the business cannot be deducted because the business has not been started yet. This is not true.
2.  Start up costs are capitalized the same way fixed assets are. However, you deduct up to $5,000 of start up costs in the first year. The amount in excess of $5,000 needs to be amortized over 180 months. Amortization is the writing off of the expense (costs) over a period of time.
3.  If the business is not started at all, then the expenses are personal and cannot be written off on your taxes.

A quick item to note, costs of organizing a company are considered organization costs and not start up costs.

## Things To Consider About Start Up Costs:

- Did you do any research for the business such as market research and location research?
- Did you pay any costs for creating a business such as advertising and consulting fees?

# Tip 14
## Tax Projections

Tax projections are a great way to see what your tax returns will look like before the end of the year.

1. Many business owners initially have business income and expenses that fluctuate from year to year. Rather than wait for tax time to find out what your tax liability will be it is advisable to complete your accounting before year-end to determine your tax liability.
2. You may find that your business has higher income than expected. If so, you can make adjustments such as:
   a. an asset purchase or pay expenses ahead of time
   b. change your withholding
   c. set up a retirement account before year end
3. There are many ways to minimize your tax liability before the year-end rather than waiting until after the year end.

**Things To Consider About Tax Projections:**

- Are there any life changes such as birth, death, marriage, or divorce?
- Are there any change in income sources such as a new business, loss of business, or additional employees?
- Are there any expiring tax laws such as tax credits?
- Consider projections for multiple years. Perhaps you can benefit by shifting income to one year for overall beneficial tax rates over two years.

# Tip 15
## Estimated Tax Payments

Estimated tax payments are taxes that are paid quarterly based on what you think you will owe. Many income sources do not have taxes withheld such as income for sole proprietorships, LLCs, and K-1s received from partnerships and S-corporations.

1. Estimated taxes are generally required to be paid if you:
   a. Owe more than $1,000
   b. Have less than 90% of the taxes due for the current year paid in throughout the current year
   c. Have less than 100% paid in of the prior year's taxes paid in for the current year
2. Estimated tax payments are due on April 15, June 15, September 15, and January 15.
3. If you are required to make estimated taxes and do not make them, you may have a penalty of 0.5% of the unpaid taxes per month. However, there may be penalty waivers available depending on your situation.

**Things To Consider About Estimated Tax Payments:**

- Are there any life changes such as  birth, death, marriage, or divorce?
- Are there any changes in income sources such as a new business, loss of business, or additional employees?

## You've finished. Before you go…

Tweet/share that you finished this book.

Please star rate this book on Amazon.

Reviews are solid gold to writers. Please take a few minutes to give us some itty bitty feedback on this book.

# ABOUT THE AUTHOR

I am a Certified Public Accountant with a practice located in Thousand Oaks, CA with over twenty five years of experience working with clients. I began my career as a bookkeeper and believe that this gives me the "inside out" experience of all levels of accounting.

I took the "long road" path of taking eighteen years to get my college degree while working a full time job and raising a family. This contributed to my belief that anybody can do what they want if they have the drive and determination.

My passion has been said to be empowering to entrepreneurs and small owners by educating them while providing personalized accounting and tax services.

I am married to my high school sweetheart, Paul. Together we have two grown sons, Richard and Robert, and two furry children, Daizy and Dozer.

DeborahAMorganCPA.com

Other Amazing Itty Bitty™ Books

- **Your Amazing Itty Bitty™ Travel Planning Book** – Rosemary Workman
- **Your Amazing Itty Bitty™ Cruise Diary** – Itty Bitty Books
- **Your Amazing Itty Bitty™ Weight Loss Book** – Suzy Prudden and Joan-Meijer-Hirschland
- **Your Amazing Itty Bitty™ Food & Exercise Log** – Suzy Prudden and Joan Meijer-Hirschland
- **Your Amazing Itty Bitty™ Astrology Book** – Carol Pilkington
- **Your Amazing Itty Bitty™ Little Black Book of Sales** – Anthony Comacho
- **Your Amazing Itty Bitty™ Safety Book** – Stephen C. Carpenter, CSP
- **Your Amazing Itty Bitty™ IRS Tax Audit Prevention Book** – Nellie T. Williams, EA

Coming Soon

- **Your Amazing Itty Bitty ™ Book of QuickBooks® ShortCuts** – Barbara Starley, CPA
- **Your Amazing Itty Bitty™ Heal Your Body Book** – Patricia Garza Pinto
- **Your Amazing Itty Bitty™ Marijuana Manual** – Kat Bohnsack

With many more Amazing Itty Bitty Books to come…

www.ingramcontent.com/pod-product-compliance
Lightning Source LLC
Chambersburg PA
CBHW071435200326
41520CB00014B/3706